GUITAR METHOD 3

Contents

Photography: Roberto Santos

Alfred Publishing Co., Inc.
16320 Roscoe Blvd., Suite 100
P.O. Box 10003
Van Nuys, CA 91410-0003
alfred.com

ISBN-10: 1-57623-290-5 (Book)
ISBN-13: 978-1-57623-290-3 (Book)
ISBN-10: 1-57623-291-3 (Book and CD)
ISBN-13: 978-1-57623-291-0 (Book and CD)

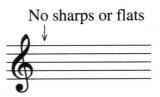

No sharps or flats

The keys of C major and A minor contain the same notes and share the same key signature (no sharps or flats). So these two keys are referred to as **relative major and minor**.

Songs in C:
- tend to center around the C note,
- usually begin and end on a C chord,
- use the G7 chord, which the ear hears as wanting to resolve (return) to C.

Songs in A minor:
- tend to center around the A note,
- usually begin and end on an A minor chord,
- use the E7 chord, which the ear hears as wanting to resolve to A.

Homeward Bound begins in C major and modulates to A minor in bar 9. This is a solo guitar arrangement with simultaneous melody and accompaniment — the melody part is written with stems up and the accompaniment is written stems down. (For a review of this concept see page 26 of *Guitar Method 2*.)

Note: This entire piece is played "arpeggio style." Hold each chord form, allowing all the notes to sustain until the next chord change. The A section is fingered in 1st position. The B section mixes open strings with 2nd position fingerings (for review see *Guitar Method 2*, page 40).

Homeward Bound

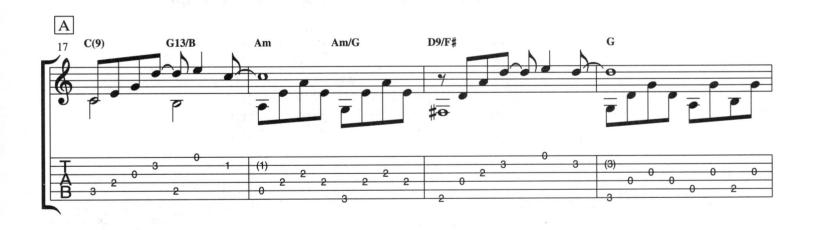

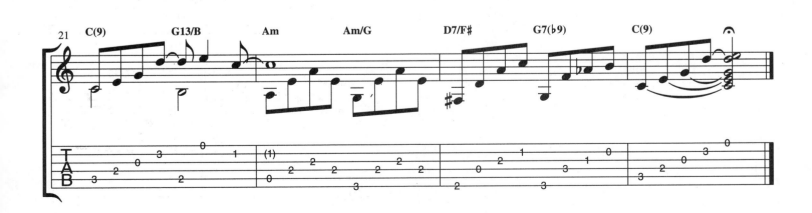

C Major/A Minor: Finger-Picking

5 Often, arpeggio-style accompaniments and solo guitar pieces (like the previous song, *Homeward Bound*) are played with the fingers instead of a pick.

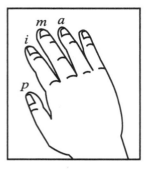

The right-hand fingers are usually indicated:

p = thumb
i = index finger
m = middle finger
a = ring finger

For each of the following examples "plant" your finger-tips on top of the strings at the beginning of each measure. Gently push each finger through the strings in a semi-circular motion that aims towards the palm of your hand.

Examples 2–4 use the I and V7 chords of the key of C (C and G7).

Ex. 2:

Ex. 3:

Ex. 4:

Examples 5–7 use the same finger-picking patterns as Examples 2–6 only now applied to the I and V7 chords in the key of A minor (Am and E7).

Ex. 5:

Ex. 6:

Ex. 7:

This next song is based on a common folk guitar chord progression. The song begins in C and then modulates to A minor at the B section. Chord frames are indicated throughout to help with the fingerings.

Country Dance

Ex. 8

*"Brush" through the chord with your thumb.

7

This is a sixteenth note:

This a sixteenth note rest:

Four sixteenth notes equal one quarter note:

In groups of two or more, sixteenth notes are beamed together:

Counting Sixteenth Notes: Sixteenth notes divide a beat into four equal parts. Count like this:

1 e & a 2 e & a 3 e & a 4 e & a

This finger-picking example is by Matteo Carcassi (1792–1853), the most famous guitar composer of his era. This exerpt from his Etude No. 7 (in A minor) should be played at a quick but very even tempo. Pay careful attention to the left- and right-hand fingerings throughout.

Ex. 9:

Etude No. 7
(Excerpt)

Carcassi

This excerpt, from Bach's Invention No. 13, begins in the key of A minor and ends in C major. Here, it is arranged as a duet to be played with a friend, teacher or the play-along recording. **Learn both parts.** This arrangement is played **pick-style** not with the fingers.

Notice the use of G♯. In the key of A minor "G" is often sharp. The G♯ leads very strongly to A and is our most important indication that we are in the key of A minor, not C major.

Note: G♯ is part of the E7 chord (E, G♯, B, D).

New Rhythm: Count the downbeat silently and play on the "e" of the beat.

Invention No. 13
(Excerpt)

Ex. 10

J. S. Bach

10 Shown below are the open and 2nd position scale fingering diagrams for the key of C (or A minor). The root note (C) for the 2nd position fingering is played by the 2nd finger, on the "A" string, so we call this fingering **"Type 2A."** Notice that the fingering temporarily shifts to the 3rd position on the 1st and 2nd strings. **Practice the Type 2A fingering until you can easily play it from memory.**

Open Position
C Scale Fingering

2nd Position, Type 2A
C Scale Fingering

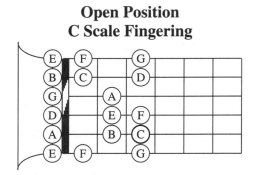
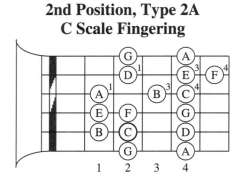

Ex. 11: C Major, Type 2A

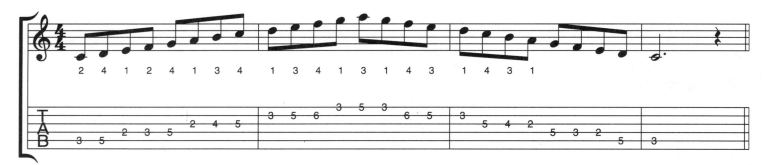

Like the moveable power chord fingerings you learned in *Guitar Method 2* (page 24), the Type 2A fingering contains no open strings, so it is a **moveable scale fingering**. To transpose this fingering to another key simply slide the entire fingering to the correct root position.

Now try transposing the Type 2A fingering to the keys of D, E, F and G. The root note for each of these keys is shown in the fretboard diagram.

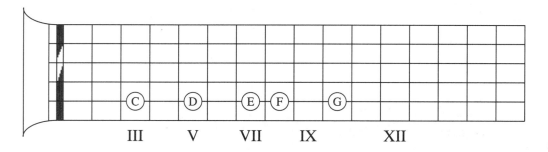

As you progress through this book you will learn five "moveable" major scale fingerings. It is essential that you memorize each. They are the key to improvising lead guitar and playing throughout the neck.

Bonaparte's Retreat is a bluegrass "flat-picking" classic and is usually played at a fast tempo. The melody spans the entire range of the 2nd position, and the long, constant 16th note melody provides excellent pick-technique practice.

Bonaparte's Retreat

Ex. 12:

In *Guitar Method 2* we converted the root ⑥ and root ⑤ power chords to moveable chord forms (for review see page 24 of *Guitar Method 2*). We will now do the same with the major, minor and dominant 7th chord forms.

To convert the root ⑥, E major chord to a moveable barre chord form:
- change the fingering and barre across all six strings with the index finger as shown,
- position the chord fingering at the correct fret — the root of the chord is under the 1st finger, on the 6th string.

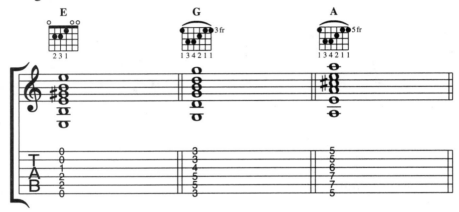

Technique: Roll your index finger to the side so the hard, outside edge of the finger forms the barre, not the soft, fleshy part of the inside.

This next example is in the style of Steve Cropper's guitar part from *(Sittin' on) the Dock of the Bay*. It is unique in that it uses only major chords.

One Chord Wonder

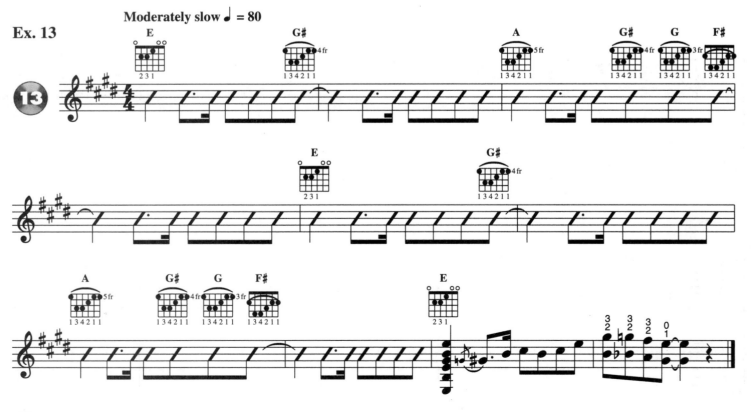

14 Now convert the open position E minor and E7 chords to moveable barre chord forms. The root of these barre chord forms is still on the sixth string.

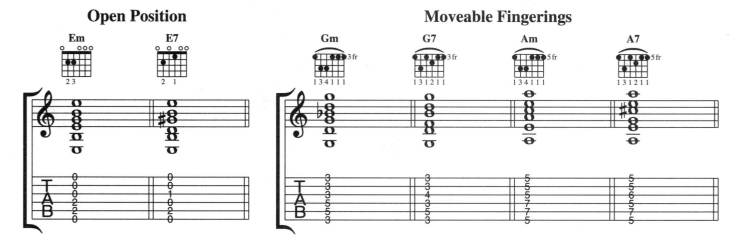

Open Position   **Moveable Fingerings**

Reminder: For strength remember to roll your index finger to the side and place your thumb firmly behind the center of the neck.

This next barre chord example uses the first five chords in the key of G: G, Am, Bm, C and D7. The example can be played with a pick or finger-style.

Barre Chord Etude No. 1

Ex. 14

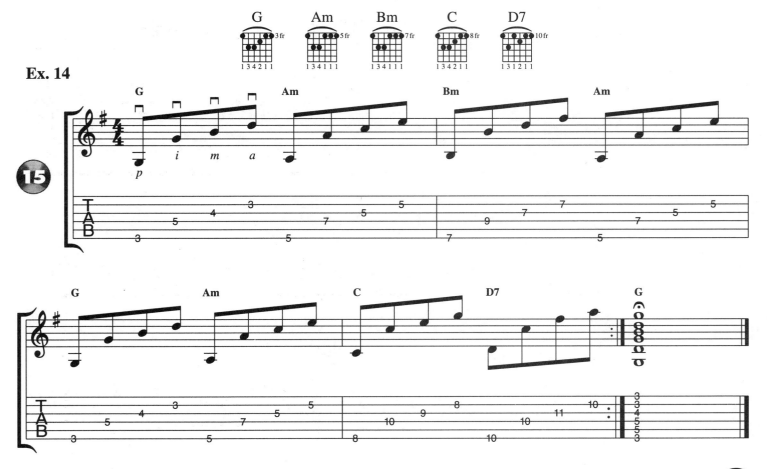

The most common lead guitar scale is the **minor pentatonic scale.** This is a five note scale ("penta" means five). Shown below is the most common fingering for this scale. Since this is a "moveable" scale pattern (6th string root) it can be transposed to any key. Here it is shown in 5th position, key of A.

A Minor Pentatonic (Root ⑥)

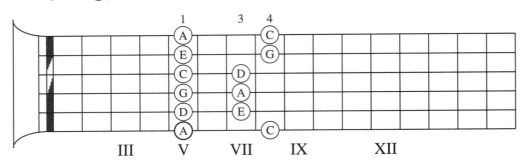

Ex. 15

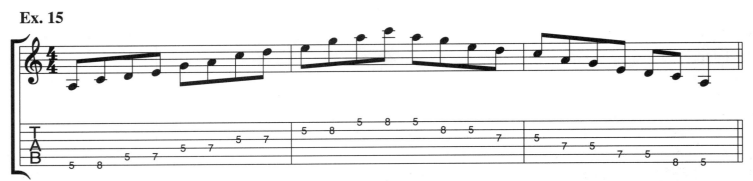

Here are four licks derived from the A minor pentatonic scale fingering. Memorize these, then try adding your own variations.

Ex. 16: Lick 1   **Ex. 17: Lick 2**

Ex. 18: Lick 3   **Ex. 19: Lick 4**

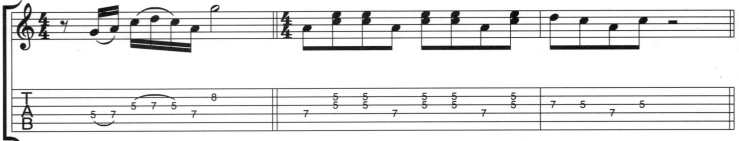

Latin Blue puts the licks and patterns from the previous page into the context of a complete solo over a "Latin" rock progression in A minor. (You'll learn the rhythm guitar part later in the book.) The whole solo is derived from the A minor pentatonic scale except for the "F" in bar 7 (from the F chord) and the G♯ in bars 10 and 11 (from the E7 chord).

On the recording, the two chord "vamp" at the end repeats for about one minute. Use this vamp to improvise your own leads.

Latin Blue
(Lead Solo)

Ex. 20

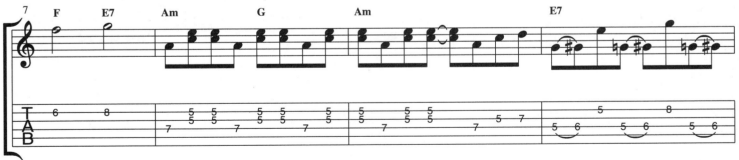

The keys of G major and E minor contain the same notes and share the same key signature (all Fs are sharp). So G major and E minor are relative major and minor.

Songs in G:
- tend to center around the G note,
- usually begin and end on a G chord,
- use the D7 chord, which the ear hears as wanting to resolve to G.

Songs in E minor:
- tend to center around the E note,
- usually begin and end on an E minor chord,
- use the B7 chord, which the ear hears as wanting to resolve to E.

This finger-picking example in the key of G is designed as a warm-up for *Country Thumpkin* on the next page, it introduces the **constant alternating bass technique**. This technique is the foundation for most finger-style guitar:
- Use the indicated fingerings.
- The thumb (*p*) plays the alternating bass pattern with a strict quarter-note pulse. You should first practice just the thumb part before adding the melody.
- The simple melody is played by the middle finger (*m*) entirely on the B string.
- Practice this example until the constant alternating thumb technique begins to feel "automatic."

Almost Thumpkin

Ex. 21

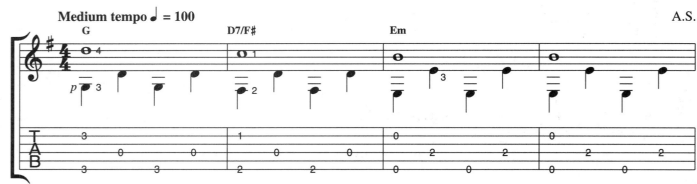

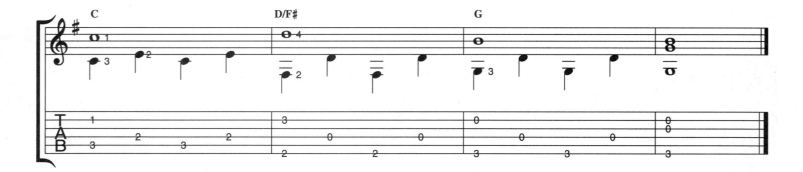

19 *Country Thumpkin* introduces the classic **Travis-Picking** pattern, named for the great country guitar pioneer, Merle Travis.

Note:
- Travis-picking is based on the constant alternating thumb technique.
- The three bass strings (played by the thumb) are usually muted by laying the palm of the right hand gently on the strings near the bridge. Hold the hand at a slight angle so as not to mute the melody played on the top three strings. When played correctly, the tonal difference between the muted bass and ringing melody can make this sound like two guitars.
- Hold the full indicated chord forms, even when all the notes are not required.
- Generally when Travis-picking, the G, B and E strings are played by the index, middle and ring fingers.
- The finger-picking pattern remains constant throughout:

```
|m      i   m   |
|p   p   p   p  |
 1 & 2 & 3 & 4 &
```

Country Thumpkin

Ex. 22

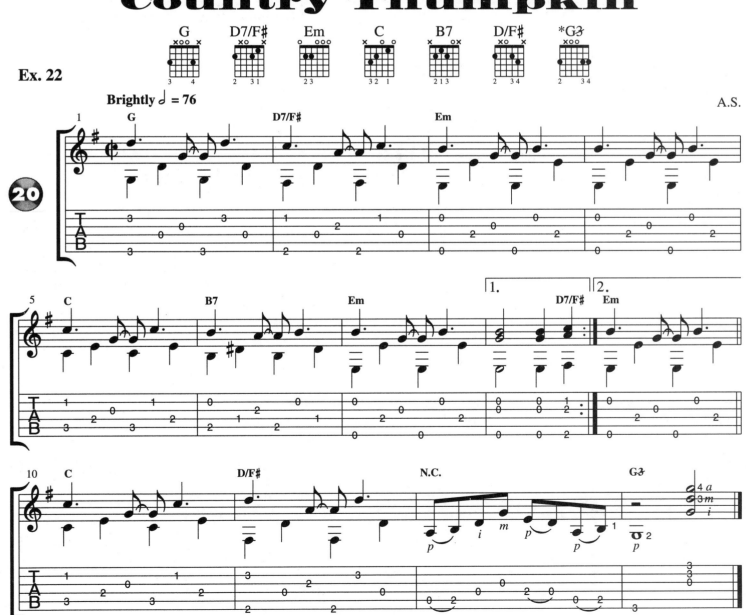

*G♩ = A G chord with no third (B).

Shown below are the open and 2nd position scale fingering diagrams for the key of G (or E minor). The root note (G) for the 2nd position "moveable" fingering is played by the 2nd finger, on the "E" string, so we call this fingering **"Type 2E."** **Practice the Type 2E fingering until you can easily play it from memory.**

**Open Position
G Scale Fingering**

**2nd Position, Type 2E
G Scale Fingering**

Ex. 23: G Major, Type 2E Fingering

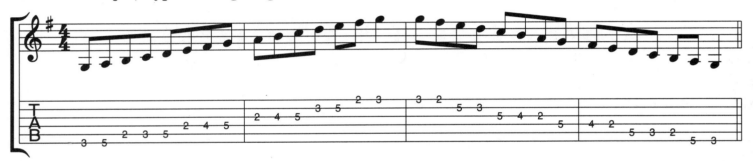

Like the type 2A fingering, the type 2E fingering contains no open strings, so it is a moveable scale fingering. To transpose this fingering to another key, simply shift the entire fingering to the correct root position. Now try transposing this fingering to the keys of A, B, C and D. The root note for each of these keys is shown in the fretboard diagram.

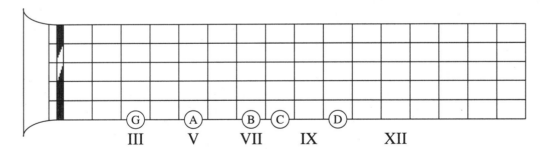

Memorizing the "moveable" major scale fingerings is an essential part of learning to play, and read music, throughout the neck. This neck diagram indicates the notes and locations of both the type 2E and 2A fingerings for the key of G. Play through both fingerings until you play them from memory.

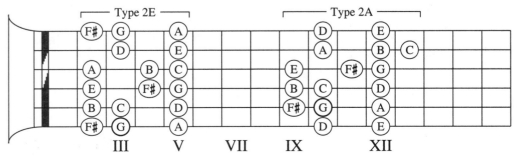

Here is an excerpt from the beginning of a Bach Prelude for Cello. It first descends, and then ascends through the entire 2nd position G scale fingering (type 2E). In bars 5 and 6 the fingering leaves the 2nd position and moves up and down the 1st string. Follow the fingering carefully.

Bach Prelude
(Excerpt)

Ex. 24

J. S. Bach

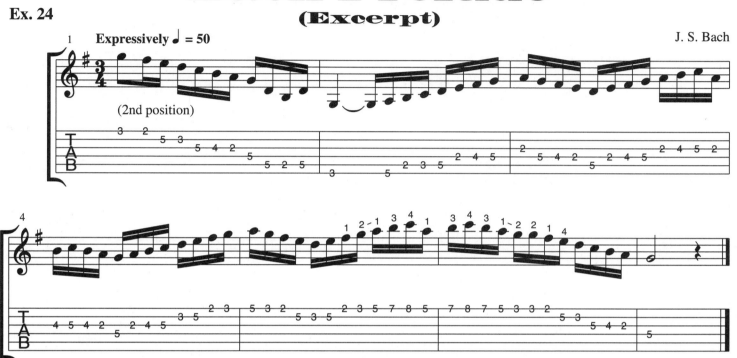

As an example of how these fingerings transpose up and down the neck, here is the Bach Prelude excerpt transposed to the key of A. For the key of A, use the type 2E fingering at the 4th position.

Bach Prelude
(Excerpt)

Ex. 25

J. S. Bach

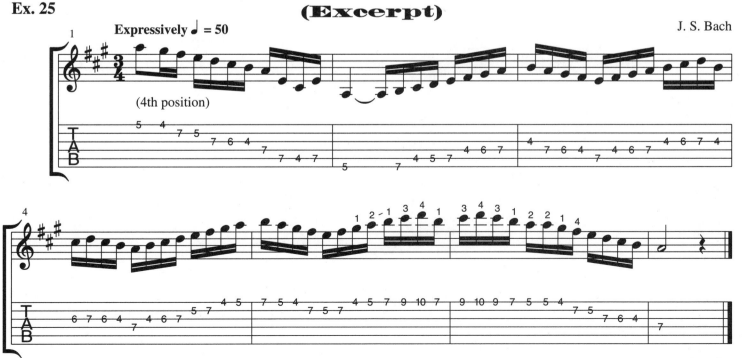

This next song uses the same 2nd position, type 2E fingering, only now the tonal center is E minor instead of G major.

Note:
- The whole song is fingered in 2nd position except bars 10–13 which shift to the 1st position.
- Even though the song is in E minor it contains no B7 chord. This is very common in traditional American and British folk music.

Bonaparte Crossing the Rocky Mountains

Ex. 26

Traditional Fiddle Tune

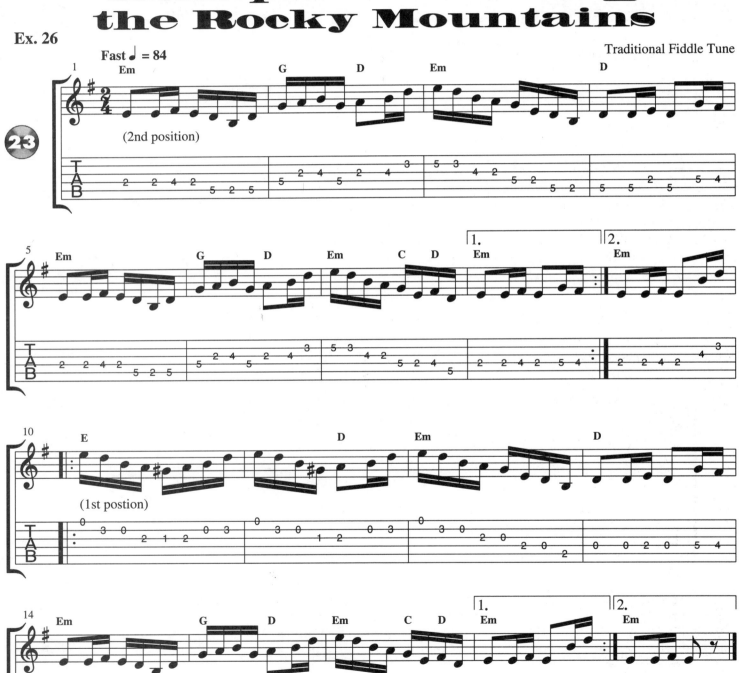

This next example uses a classical finger-picking technique of having the thumb play a melody (in this case a G scale, written with stems down) against a constant, repeated-note "E" played by the fingers (written stems up). The open E can be played by the index finger alone, or by alternating the index and middle. Try both techniques.

Ex. 27

My Spanish Thumb uses the previous finger-picking technique. I've fingered the song with a mixture of 2nd position and open string notes to give it a ringing harp-like quality. The song ends with an E minor chord played in **harmonics**. Gently touch your left-hand ring finger to the top three strings directly over the 12th fret, do not press down. Strike the three strings with your thumb and immediately release your ring finger from the strings. You should hear a ringing bell-like sound known as harmonics.

My Spanish Thumb

Ex. 28 Moderately ♩ = 88

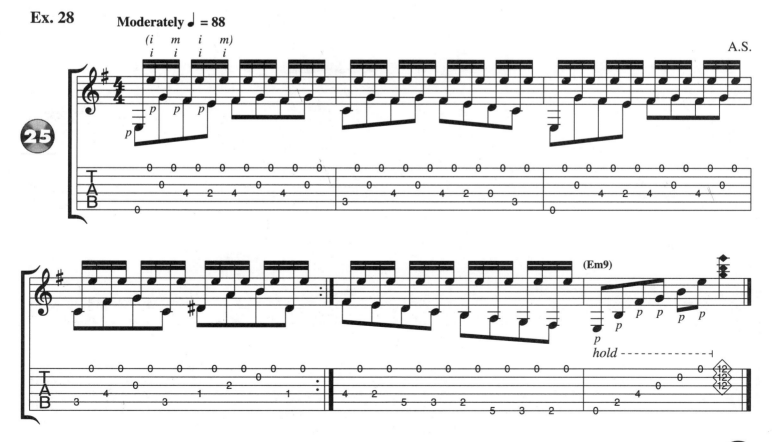

G Major/E Minor: Guitar Rag

26 *Guitar Rag* combines the Travis-picking technique with some 2nd position finger-ings. Note that:

- The most important element of this technique is the constant alternating bass. To increase the separation between melody and bass mute the bottom strings with the palm of your right hand.
- The song can be played with a swing feel (in the country-blues style) or a straight eighth feel (like a Scott Joplin rag). Both feels are demonstrated on the recording.
- The whole song is built on a single, two-measure, finger-picking pattern. Hold the indicated chord for each two-measure phrase and apply this pattern:

Practice this example before attempting the whole song:

Ex. 29

Guitar Rag

Ex. 30

27

28 To convert the root ⑤ A major chord to a moveable barre chord form:

- change the fingering and barre across the first five strings with the index finger as shown,
- position the chord fingering at the correct fret — the root of the chord is under the 1st finger, on the 5th string.

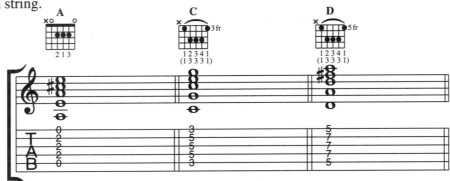

Technique: The notes on the three middle strings can be played with either your 2nd, 3rd, and 4th fingers or a 3rd finger barre. If you use a 3rd finger barre make sure to arch your finger so that it doesn't interfere with the 1st string.

This example is based on the Kinks' "You Really Got Me" and was covered by Van Halen on their debut recording. The song uses just the moveable root ⑤ major barre chord form.

Ex. 31

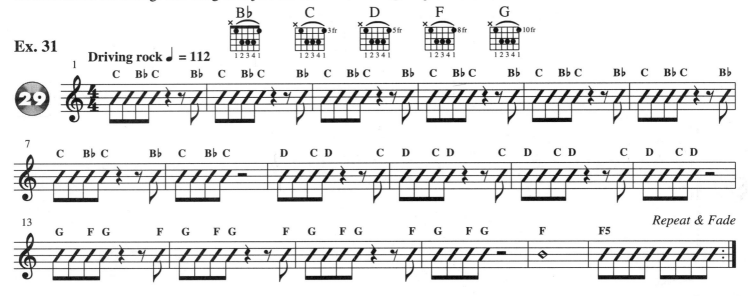

30 This next example is one of the most common rock and roll chord riffs and uses both the root ⑥ and root ⑤ major chord forms. The rhythm used in Example 32A is similar to *Louie, Louie.* Example 32B uses the same chord progression but with a rhythm similar to *Twist and Shout* or *La Bamba.*

Ex. 32A

Ex. 32B

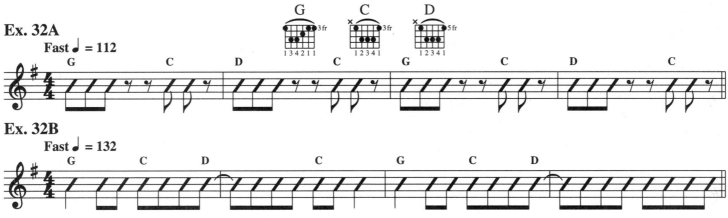

31 Now convert the open position A minor and A7 chords to moveable barre chord forms. Again, the root of these chord forms is on the fifth string.

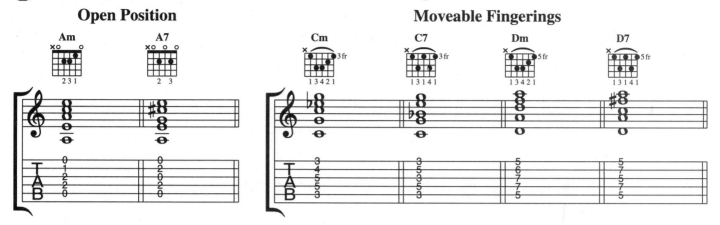

On page 13 you learned a lead guitar solo to "Latin Blue." Here is the rhythm guitar part. It uses each of the barre chord forms. Notice the small grace note "D" in the opening lick. A grace note is played very fast and has no rhythmic value of its own. This one is played on beat 3 and immediately slurred to "E."

Latin Blue
(Rhythm Guitar)

Ex. 33

Latin rock ♩ = 100

A.S.

Repeat & Fade

Hotel California

There are three guitar parts in this arrangement: Gtr. 1 plays the arpeggio part, Gtr. 2 plays the melody and the ending solo and Gtr. 3 plays the strumming part using only barre chords.

Note:
- The classic arpeggio intro to *Hotel California* uses basic "open" position chord forms and can be played either finger-style or with a pick.
- The intro figure continues throughout the song. At the Chorus apply the same arpeggio pattern to the new chords.
- The melody should be played in 2nd position using the G major, type 2E fingering. No tab is indicated for the melody.
- The strumming part (Gtr. 3) begins at the Verse and continues throughout the song.
- The ending solo can also be played either finger- or pick-style. The solo consists of arpeggios derived from the root ⑤ and root ⑥ barre chord forms.

Hotel California

Ex. 34

Words and Music by
DON HENLEY, GLENN FREY
and DON FELDER

Verse 2:
Her mind is Tiffany twisted.
She got her Mercedes Bends.
She got a lot of pretty, pretty boys
That she calls friends.
How they dance in the courtyard;
Sweet summer sweat.
Some dance to remember;
Some dance to forget.

So I called up the captain:
"Please bring me my wine."
He said, "We haven't had that spirit here
Since nineteen sixty-nine."
And still those voices are calling from far away;
Wake you up in the middle of the night
Just to hear them say:
(To Chorus:)

34 The ability to bend notes is one of the most unique characteristics of the guitar. All of the following examples are derived from the 5th position A minor pentatonic scale. The fretboard diagram illustrates three whole-step bends.

A Minor Pentatonic:

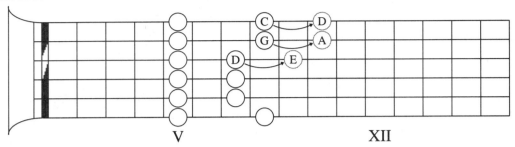

Example 35A shows a slide from D to E on the 3rd string. Play this several times to get the sound of D moving to E in your ear, then try the bend in 35B. To check your intonation, repeatedly play the fretted E and then the bent E, checking to make sure the bent pitch matches that of the fretted note.

Ex. 35A   **Ex. 35B**

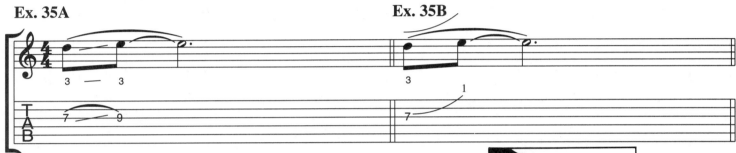

Technique: Place your 1st and 2nd fingers directly behind your 3rd finger. Use all three fingers to push the string up (towards the sky). You should also hook your thumb over the top of the neck and "squeeze" the string between your thumb and fingers, this will add a lot of strength to your hand.

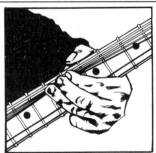

Examples 36 and 37 show whole step bends on the 2nd and 1st strings. You can use either the 3rd or 4th finger for this bend. Either way, support the bend with your remaining fingers.

Ex. 36A   **Ex. 36B**

Ex. 37A   **Ex. 37B**

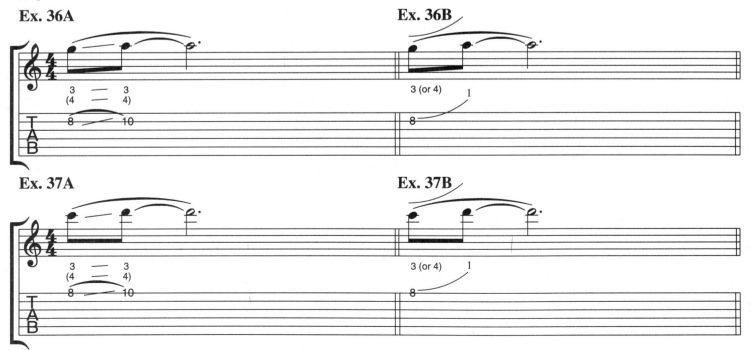

In each of the previous bend examples, the fretted note had a definite rhythmic value. Often bends are played so fast the fretted note has no rhythmic value. When this is the case the fretted note is indicated with a cue size (small) note head as in the following example. Play the fretted note, then immediately bend to the indicated pitch.

Ex. 38A   **Ex. 38B**   **Ex. 38C**

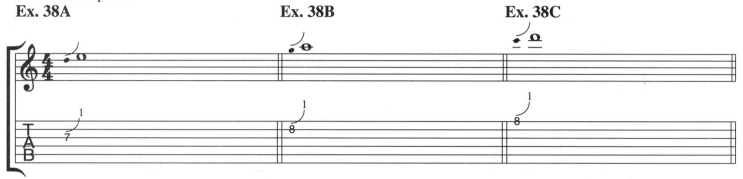

Example 39 shows some typical "**Bend and Return**" licks. Play the fretted note, immediately bend to the indicated pitch, then release the bend back down to the original note. Only the first note is attacked with the pick.

Ex. 39A   **Ex. 39B**   **Ex. 39C**

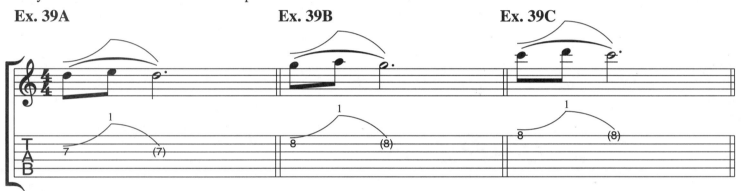

This next lick features a very common technique — a bend and return followed immediately by a pull-off. On the 3rd string, bend D to E, release back down to D then pull-off to C. Example 40B shows the same lick played in a repetitive pattern.

Ex. 40A   **Ex. 40B**

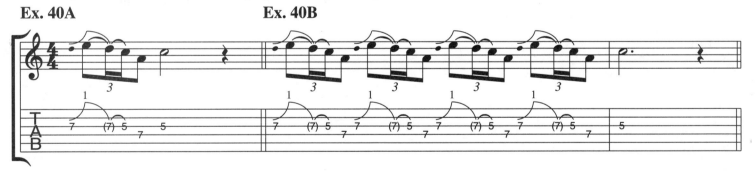

For Example 41 barre your 1st finger across the 1st and 2nd strings, with your 3rd and 2nd fingers bend 3rd string D to E. The lick ends with a bend from G to A.

Ex. 41

It is very important that you learn to play all these moveable scales, licks and patterns in every key/every position. This next example, based on two of the bending licks from the previous page, begins in G minor (3rd position minor pentatonic scale) and modulates up the neck to B♭ minor, C minor, D minor, and finally G minor again, one octave higher than the starting point. **The pattern stays the same, only its position on the neck changes.** Learn both the rhythm and lead parts.

36

Move it on Up

Shuffle rock ♩ = 100

A.S.

Ex. 42

(Cont. rhythm simile)

37 The keys of D major and B minor contain the same notes and share the same key signature (all Fs and Cs are sharp). So D major and B minor are relative major and minor.

Songs in D:
- tend to center around the D note,
- usually begin and end on a D chord,
- use the A7 chord, which the ear hears as wanting to resolve to D.

Songs in B minor:
- tend to center around the B note,
- usually begin and end on a B minor chord,
- use the F#7 chord, which the ear hears as wanting to resolve to B.

This pick-style solo guitar arrangement of "Greensleeves" is in B minor and uses the moveable root ⑤ and ⑥ barre chord forms to harmonize the melody. The top note of each chord is a melody note. The other melody notes are either part of the chord form or are easily played with your remaining fingers while holding down the chord.

"Greensleeves" introduces the 6/8 time signature:

6 = Six Beats Per Measure
8 = The Eighth Note Receives One Beat

6/8 "feels" like 2/4 with the quarter note pulse divided into eighth note triplets:

Greensleeves

Ex. 43

Anonymous

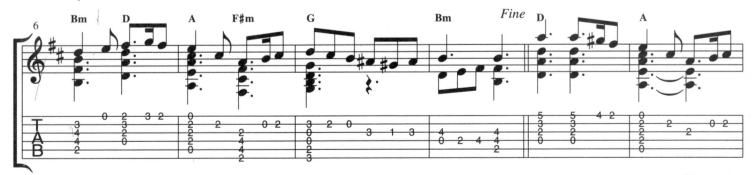

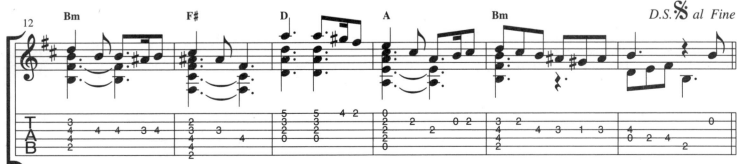

Shown below are the open and 2nd position scale fingering diagrams for the key of D (or B minor). The root note (D) for the moveable fingering is played by the 4th finger, on the "A" string so we call this fingering **"Type 4A."** Practice the Type **4A fingering until you can easily play it from memory.**

**Open Position
D Scale Fingering**

**2nd Position, Type 4A
D Scale Fingering**

Ex. 44: D Major, Type 4A Fingering

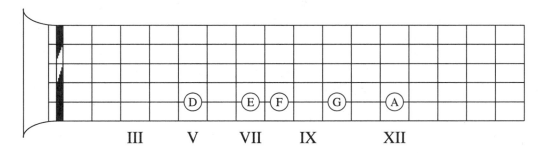

Like the type 2A and 2E fingerings, the type 4A fingering contains no open strings, so it is a moveable scale fingering. To transpose this fingering to another key, simply shift the entire fingering to the correct root position. Now try transposing this fingering to the keys of E, F, G and A. The root note for each of these keys is shown in the fretboard diagram.

Again, memorizing the "moveable" major scale fingerings is an essential part of learning to play, and read music, throughout the neck. This neck diagram indicates, for the key of D, the notes and locations of three fingerings you have learned so far. Play through each fingering until you can play them from memory.

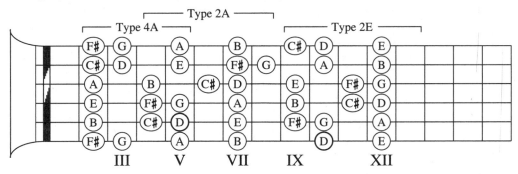

This excerpt from the ending of the Prelude from J.S. Bach's "First Cello Suite," is arranged to be played with a pick.

Note:
- The fingering for measures 1 and 2 is derived from the 2nd position, type 4A, D major fingering.
- In measures 3 and 4 the eighth-note melody (stems down) alternates with a constant open "E" pedal tone (stems up).
- In measures 5–9 the melody (still stems down) is a simple D major scale pattern played almost entirely on the "G" string. Again, this melody alternates with a constant open "E" pedal tone.
- In measures 9 and 10 the melody changes from D major scale patterns to a chromatic scale (chromatic means every note, every fret). This chromatic scale melody first moves up the "B" string to the 7th position and then switches to the "E" string, still in 7th position.
- Notice the 12th fret "A" harmonic in measures 5 and 6. Touch the 5th string directly above the 12th fret, strike the string and immediately release your finger. You will hear a ringing harmonic.
- The climax of the piece is played by arpeggiating through three simple chord fingerings in the 7th position. See the tablature for the fingerings.
- The piece should be played with alternate picking. In measure 9 the down-up pattern reverses to up-down until the D chord in measure 11.

Prelude (Excerpt)
(From the First Cello Suite)

Ex. 45

J. S. Bach

Moderately ♩ = 60

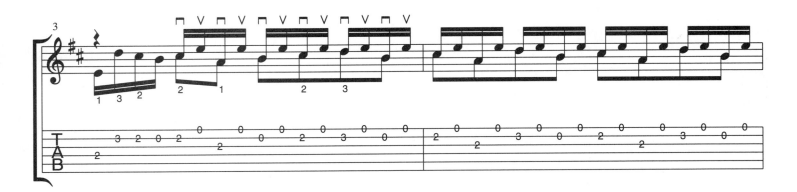

A Major/F♯ Minor: Way Cool Guitar

42 The keys of A major and F♯ minor contain the same notes and share the same key signature (F, C and G are sharp). So A major and F♯ minor are relative major and minor. A major is a very popular guitar key. F♯ minor is not as common.

Songs in A:
- tend to center around the A note,
- usually begin and end on an A chord,
- use the E7 chord, which the ear hears as wanting to resolve to A.

Songs in F♯ minor:
- tend to center around the F♯ note,
- usually begin and end on an F♯ minor chord,
- use the C♯7 chord, which the ear hears as wanting to resolve to F♯.

Way Cool Guitar is built around a driving rock boogie pattern in A; which has been the predominant rock and roll key since Chuck Berry laid down the rock and roll foundation back in the fifties. The song is fingered in 2nd position although the low E, A and D notes are played open. Follow the left-hand fingerings carefully. To get the correct feel, use all down-strokes and play with a palm mute throughout.

Way Cool Guitar

Ex. 46   Fast ♩ = 152   A.S.

Shown below are the open and 2nd position scale fingering diagrams for the key of A (or F♯ minor). The root note (A) for the moveable fingering is played by the 4th finger, on the "E" string, so we call this fingering **"Type 4E." Practice the Type 4E fingering until you can easily play it from memory.**

**Open Position
A Scale Fingering**

**2nd Position, Type 4E
A Scale Fingering**

Ex. 47: A Major, Type 4E Fingering

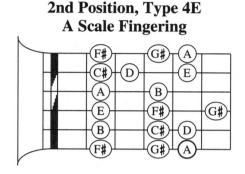

Like the three previous fingerings, the type 4E fingering contains no open strings, so it is a moveable scale fingering. To transpose this fingering to another key, simply shift the entire fingering to the correct root position. Now try transposing this fingering to the keys of B, C, D and E. The root note for each of these keys is shown in the fretboard diagram.

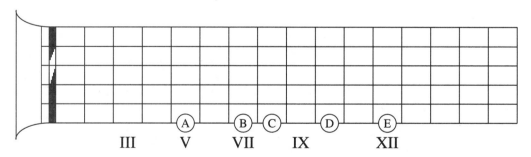

This neck diagram indicates, for the key of A, the notes and locations of the four fingerings you have learned so far. Play through each fingering until you can play them from memory.

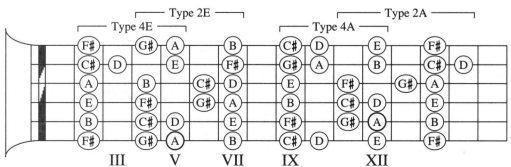

35

45 *Bill Cheatham* is a fast bluegrass tune in A. The fingering lies perfectly in 2nd position using the "Type 4E" fingering.

Note:
- The song is in 2/4.
- Because of the many consecutive notes fingered at the 2nd fret, you may want to keep your index finger in a relaxed barre position over the middle strings at the 2nd fret through much of the piece, this will eliminate the need to move the index finger too rapidly.
- Measures 11 and 15 move temporarily to the 4th position.
- Practice playing the accompaniment part using both open position and barre chord forms. Use a bass/chord type pattern as shown below.

Ex. 48

Bill Cheatham

Ex. 49

A major is an ideal key for finger-picking blues because the bass note of each chord in the A blues progression is an open string (A, D, E). *Bluesfinger* is similar to the classic finger-picking "country blues" patterns of Robert Johnson, Mississippi John Hurt or Blind Boy Fuller.

Note:
- The open-string bass notes are played with the right-hand thumb.
- The two-note chords are played with the index and ring fingers.
- The left-hand fingerings are indicated above the notation.
- The song ends on a jazz-like A13 chord. See the notes and tab for the fingering.

Bluesfinger

Ex. 50

48 The keys of F major and D minor contain the same notes and share the same key signature (all "B" notes are flat). So F major and D minor are relative major and minor.

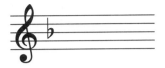

Songs in F:
- tend to center around the F note,
- usually begin and end on an F chord,
- use the C7 chord, which the ear hears as wanting to resolve to F.

Songs in D minor:
- tend to center around the D note,
- usually begin and end on a D minor chord,
- use the A7 chord, which the ear hears as wanting to resolve to D.

Black and White Rag is a traditional country rag in the key of F. A "rag" is usually played with swing eighth notes (♪♪ = ♪³♪). The whole arrangement works well in open position.

Black and White Rag

Ex. 51

Western swing ♩ = 126 (♪♪ = ♪³♪)

Traditional Fiddle Tune

This is an excellent classical finger-style study in D minor. The whole piece is based on a few simple finger-picking patterns which are then applied to every chord in the song.

Caprice in D Minor

Ex. 52

Carcassi

Medium tempo ♩ = 60

F Major/D Minor: Exploring the Neck

51 The root note (F) for the moveable fingering is played by the 1st finger, on the "E" string, so we call this fingering **"Type 1E."** Notice this fingering begins with a 1st finger "stretch." Place your hand in 2nd position and reach back to the 1st fret "F" with your index finger. Also, the fingering moves temporarily to the 3rd position on the 1st and 2nd strings. **Practice the Type 1E fingering until you can easily play it from memory.**

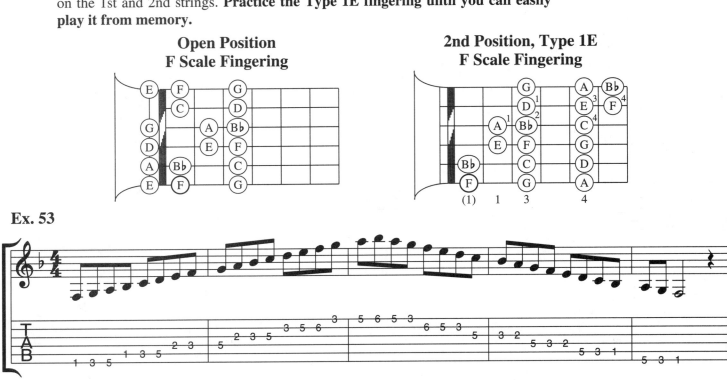

Ex. 53

Like the four previous fingerings, the type 1E fingering contains no open strings, so it is a moveable scale fingering. To transpose this fingering to another key, simply shift it to the correct root position. Now try transposing this fingering to the keys of G, A, B and C. The root note for each of these keys is shown in the fretboard diagram.

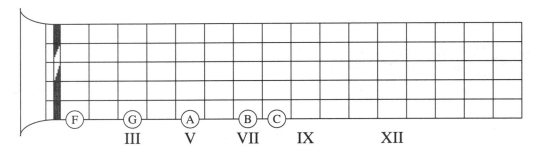

This neck diagram indicates, for the key of F, the notes and locations of the five fingerings you have now learned. Play through each fingering until you can play them from memory.

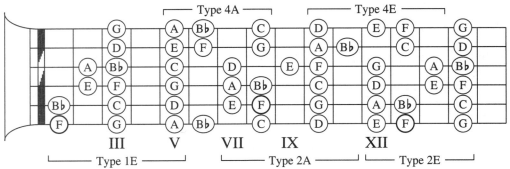

Czardas is a well known Hungarian melody.

Note:
- The song is in 2/4 (two beats per measure).
- The key is D minor. The F Type 1E fingering works with the addition of some C#
  notes.
- The fast 16th note lines make this a great speed-picking study.

Czardas

Ex. 54

Monti

53 Here are the five moveable major scale fingerings, each shown in the key of C. These five fingerings are the key to playing throughout the entire neck of the guitar.

Note:
- As you move from one fingering to the next you traverse the entire neck.
- As you progress up the neck the fingerings follow this sequence: 2A-4E-2E-1E-4A
- After the last fingering the cycle begins all over again: 2A-4E-2E-1E-4A-2A-4E-etc. So, after the type 4A fingering, the next fingering would be type 2A at the 14th position, one octave higher than the starting point.
- These fingerings can be applied to any key. For example, beginning in 2nd position the fingerings for the keys of G, D, A and F would be:

> Key of G: 2E-1E-4A-2A-4E-2E-etc.
> Key of D: 4A-2A-4E-2E-1E-4A-etc.
> Key of A: 4E-2E-1E-4A-2A-4E-etc.
> Key of F: 1E-4A-2A-4E-2E-1E-etc.

Play through each fingering until you can play them easily from memory then play them for the keys of G, D, A and F.

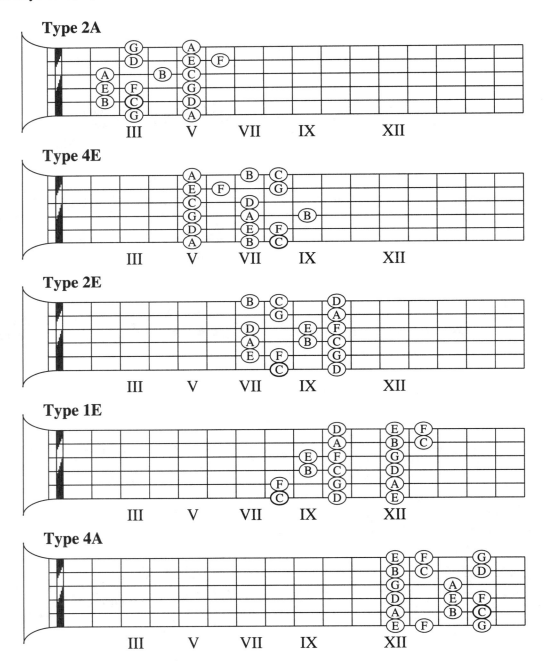

Here are the five fingerings indicated on one fretboard diagram for the key of C. Notice that the cycle begins to repeat with the Type 2A fingering at the 14th position.

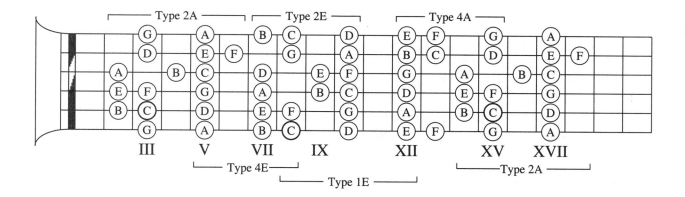

This reading study traverses the entire neck. Work through this slowly. Carefully follow the indicated fingerings and position shifts.

Reading Study

Ex. 55

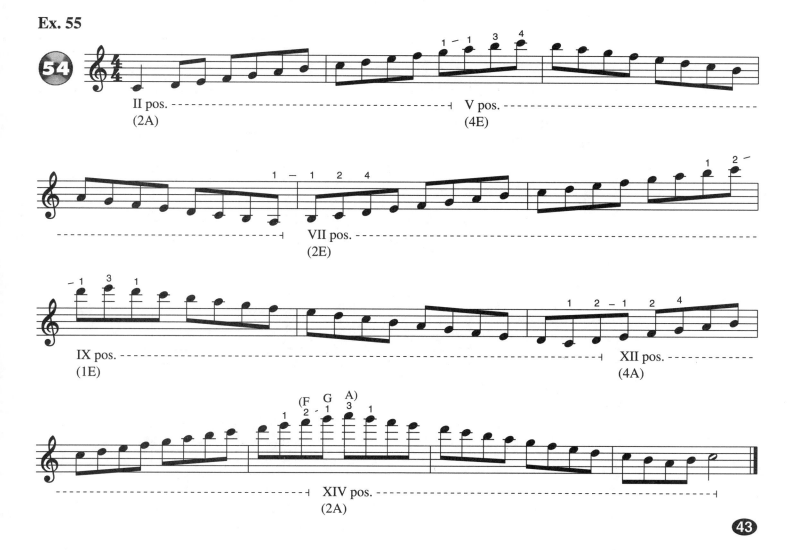

In this last section we'll see how everything you've learned so far is utilized in Jimmy Page's guitar parts to *Stairway to Heaven*. Here we'll be examining just the six main guitar figures.

Note:
- The song is in A minor.
- Section A is a finger-style part that serves as both the introduction and the background for the first two verses.
- Notes written stems down are played by the thumb, stems up by the fingers.

Stairway to Heaven

Words and Music by
JIMMY PAGE and ROBERT PLANT

Ex. 56

56 Section B is the introduction to Verses 3–6. The Em, D and C chords in measures 3 and 4 are actually the top three notes of the standard Root ⑤ barre chord forms. This part is played with a pick.

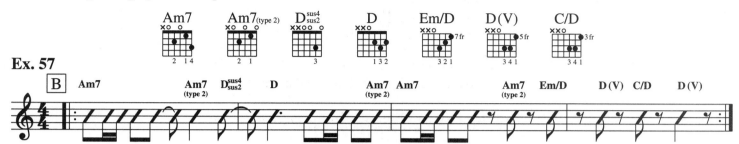

Ex. 57

57 Section C is the next verse figure. This part is followed by B each time it is played.

Ex. 58

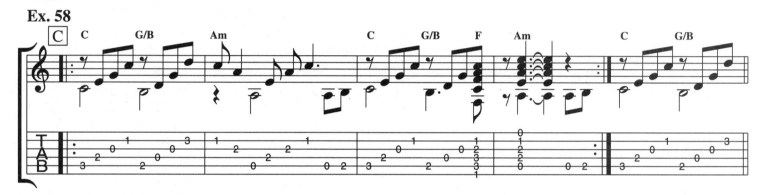

58 Section D is the transition to the guitar solo. This part is great strumming practice and is extremely syncopated.

Ex. 59

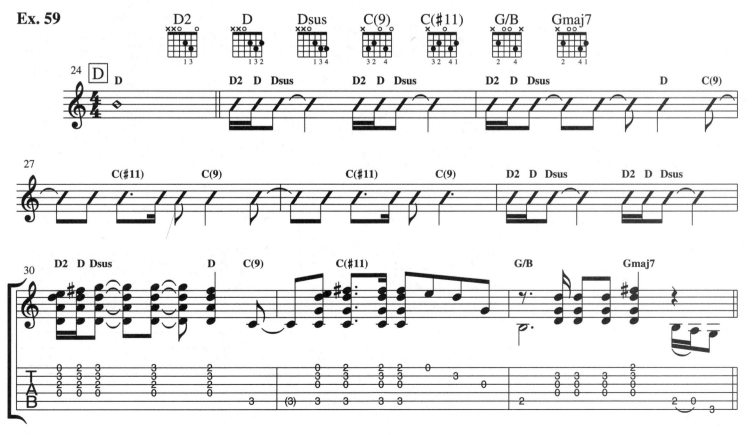

Stairway to Heaven

 The fingerings for Jimmy Page's guitar solo are drawn completely from the A minor (same as C major) and A pentatonic minor scales. Learning this solo will put you well on your way towards playing rock lead guitar.

Note:
- Bars 1–7 are played almost entirely in the 5th position using the A minor pentatonic scale fingering.
- Bars 8–17 are marked *8va.* This means to play one octave higher than written. Bars 8–13 are played in the 12th position. The 12th position A minor fingering is the same as C type 4A. Bars 14 and 15 are in the 17th position. Don't let this throw you. It's the same as 5th position only one octave (12 frets) higher.
- The repeated bend lick in bars 9, 10 and 11 is very similar to the lick you learned on page 28. Listen to the recording and you'll get the feel.

Ex. 60

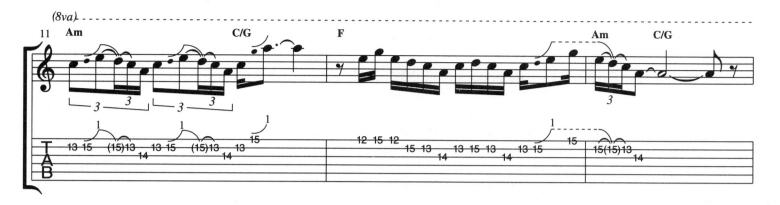

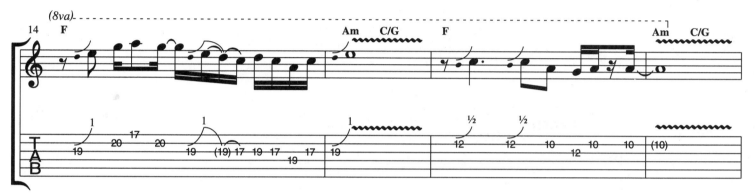

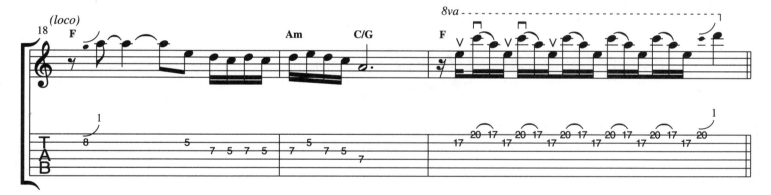

The final section of *Stairway to Heaven* is based on a heavily accented 16th note strum pattern. The x's indicate muted strums. Release the left-hand pressure on the muted chords so that only a percussive "click" sound is produced.

Ex. 61

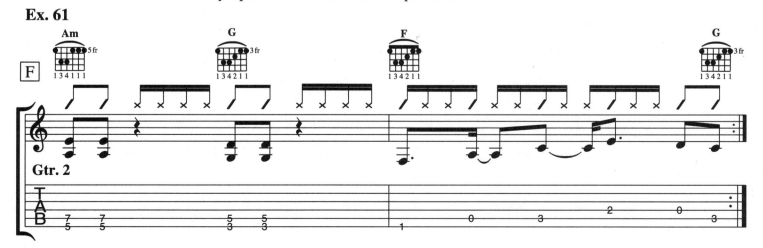

Guitar Fingerboard Chart

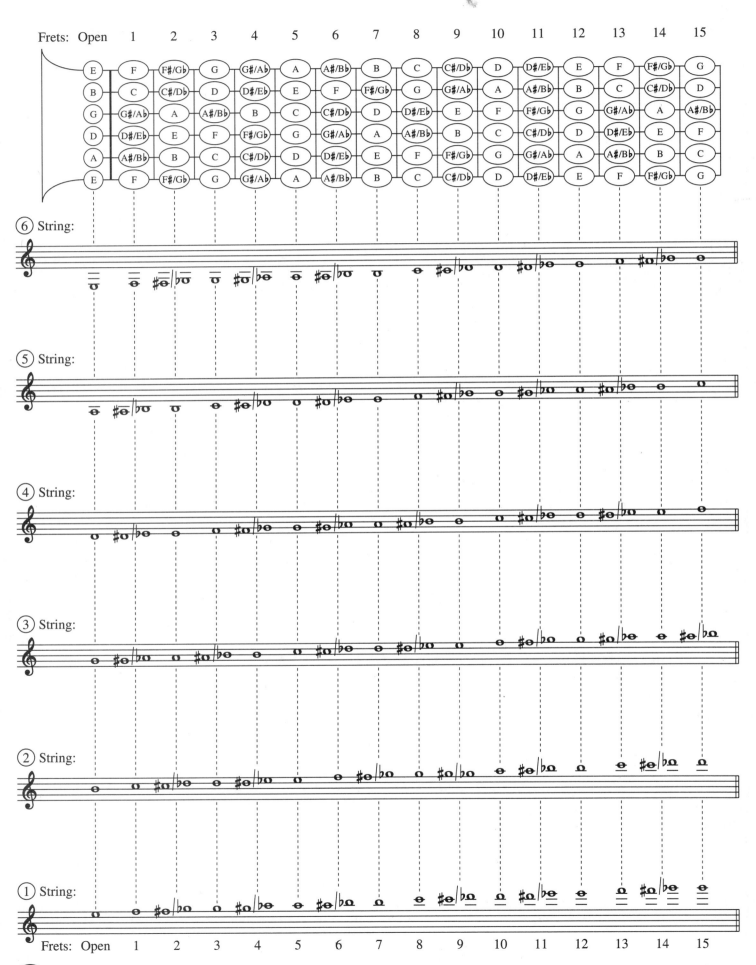